Family Matters

Poems for and about Grandparents and Grandchildren

Family Matters

Poems for and about Grandparents and Grandchildren

by

Judie Rae

© 2023 Judie Rae. All rights reserved.
This material may not be reproduced in any form, published,
reprinted, recorded, performed, broadcast,
rewritten or redistributed without
the explicit permission of Judie Rae.
All such actions are strictly prohibited by law.

Cover design by Shay Culligan
Author's and grandmother's photo by George Hatch

ISBN: 978-1-63980-353-8

Kelsay Books
502 South 1040 East, A-119
American Fork, Utah 84003
Kelsaybooks.com

*These poems are dedicated to the grandmothers and grandchildren
who enrich each other's lives.*

*Special gratitude to my grandchildren,
Hannah, Colton, Aubrey, and Chloe,
who so enrich mine.*

*Also dedicated to the memory of my grandmother,
Hettie Hatch,
who gave me a childhood to remember.*

Acknowledgments

Thank you to the following publications, where versions of these poems previously appeared:

The Acorn: "Geese on a Northern California Pond"
Albatross: "Turn of Hand"
Canary: "Geese on a Northern California Pond"
Current: "What We Have Wrought," "The Woodshed"
Howling Down the Moon (Finishing Line Press): "The Test of Time," "Why I Am a Vegetarian," "The Corset," "Stitching a Life"
Inscape: "Country Hands," "Dentist Appointment"
Kaleidoscope: "Dentist Appointment"
Lighten Up Online: "A Strange Repast" as "The Salad"
Nimrod: "The Quickening"
Sanskrit: "The Corset"
The Weight of Roses (Finishing Line Press): "Aubrey at One," "The Quickening," "Taking Back the Moon," "Geese on a Northern California Pond"
When the Virus Came Calling (Golden Foothills Press): "Bringing Her Home"

With special thanks to good friends—and great poets—Judy Brackett Crowe and Ellen Reynard, for their help and wise counsel.

And thanks to Richard Hill for enhancing the cover photo.

Contents

The Cottage	13
What She Said	15
The Ottawa	16
Country Hands	18
Grandma's Braids	19
The Corset	21
A Strange Repast	24
Sunday Mornings	26
A Lesson in Stoicism	28
Good Neighbors	29
Bringing Her Home	30
The Woodshed	32
Unspoken Love	33
Geese on a Northern California Pond	35
Simple Gifts	36
Taking Back the Moon	37
Directions to the Good Life	39
Stitching a Life	40
The Quickening	42
For Aubrey, at One	43
T-Rex Rebuke	44
From the Mouths of Babes	45
More Than His Share	46
Saving for College	47
In Aubrey's Shadow	48
Why I Am a Vegetarian	50
Family Ties	51
Almost Here	52
Lies We Tell Children	53
The Environmentalist	54
All For One	55
Dentist Appointment	56
Equine Love	58

Walkaway	59
The Test of Time	60
Climbing Mount Hope	63
The Grandmother I Never Knew	64
A Grace Note	66
Sweeping Up a Life	68
What We Have Wrought	69
Two Gardeners	71
Turn of Hand	72

The Cottage

No one clear memory
of the first time I saw my grandmother's
cottage stands out, no haunting view that returns
distinct from all the other times
I visited—and loved—that home.

The river? Certainly that. But also
the wooden kitchen floor Grandma
painted forest green,
bent over at the waist, wearing her
no-nonsense shoes.

The washer with the wringer
that once drew her hand through.
The bruises, the broken
hand, I see still.

Her garden: the raspberries
fresh on cereal
or ice cream, the tiny bug
I found floating
in the melted dessert.
He didn't eat much,
she told me.

The dining room where
we sat together and watched
summer storms gather
over the Ottawa, the thunder,
the lightning as vivid
as today's downpours
3000 miles away.

The Canada Geese
in flocks overhead
flying south, a reminder
that our summer stay
would soon end.
The cottage is gone now,
torn down with others along
the road to make a park
for visitors to enjoy,

though none treasured
that magic place
more than that child
long gone, whose
remembrance is
a gift from a woman
long gone, who remains
in memory
in the cottage
by the water.

What She Said

I can hear still my grandmother's
archaic language, feel her warm
aged hands as she patted my back,
attempting to soothe me,

to erase the pain of whatever
hurt had befallen her grandchild.
Solace was her magic,
a stoic's take on the world,
the bandage she offered.

Her own pain was masked,
lessened
by the aid she gave
others.

While I railed at the injustices
of the world directed right at me,
she nodded
and rubbed my shoulders
waiting for the ache
to ease, listening,
always listening, saying
little, though some words
ring yet in memory:

Don't fret, child.

The Ottawa

That child who sat
by the river
saw the waterway
through the eyes of possibility:
hope, adventure, excitement,
and calm were all present
in the gentle ripples
licking the shore,
in the minnows
exploring her toes.

Freedom, too,
was yards away
from the cottage
where her grandmother
cooked, gardened, knitted
her way through humid
Canadian summers,
while the child
strolled the beach,
searched for treasures
beyond value,
perfect pebbles
to line her pockets
until the next
skipping contest
with the neighbor kids.

Who knew then,
that her grandmother's gift
of the river,
of its solitude and beauty
would be a lifelong bounty,
one that laps still
as alive and fresh
as those years long past?

Country Hands

Her hands were country hands,
fashioned to coax growth from barren land.
Impervious to thorn, to burn of sun,
her hands bore nettle's sting, spider's tongue,
to pluck promises from unforgiving earth.

Her hands could draw fire where others failed,
could ease a nervous cat through summer storm,
or lift a naked bird—all beak and veins—back
to fragile nest.

Hammers knew her touch.
The glider she mended
swings yet on memory's porch
as lazy, as constant, as
an insect's hum.

Callused hands,
scarred hands,
bled into earth,
returned in a thousand acts
all that was reaped.

Humble hands.

My grandmother's hands,
hard as aged wood,
pat yet the small of my back,
reach beyond time in patient rhythm
to calm a troubled child.

Country hands.
Her polish was toil,
her toughened nails,
a scratched, but placid gift.

Grandma's Braids

Summer mornings at the cottage
if I woke early,
Grandma would let me
brush her hair before she arranged it for the day.
Her gray tresses, falling to her waist,
were fine and yellowed with age.
A careful child, I was cautious not to pull or yank.

After I finished my task,
Grandma would part her locks
down the middle, then braid
her hair by feel, finally
winding both halves
into a no-nonsense bun
held tight with hairpins.

I asked her once
why her hair remained
untrimmed.
"Tom asked me long ago
never to cut it," she said. "So I never did."
Tears warmed her eyes as she spoke
of her husband, dead before I was born.

Years later I shared her story
with the help at the rest home,
people eager to make their jobs easier,
eager to cut off
my grandmother's hair.

I resumed my old pleasure,
showed them how
to "get the tats out,"
showed them how
to garner her favor.

They fought her.
She fought them,
but went to her grave,
her promise to Tom
upheld,
her lovely locks intact.

The Corset

my grandmother wore
could stand upright,
the stays so rigid I could feel
them through the house dresses
she favored.
I'd touch not flesh
but substance as unswerving
as she.

Every morning
was the same—
even during the heat
of Canadian summers
she'd rise,
fasten with rheumatic fingers
the endless hooks.

I'd watch, a bean-pole child,
as she strapped her ample body
into the straitlaced
straitjacket, leaning over
to arrange her large breasts
so they conformed
to the outline of her confinement.

Next, she'd attach
stockings to the garters
that hung like sleeping
insects around the base
of her girdle.

In a shallow bowl
on her dresser lay
extra stays, bone people
I played with, marching their sturdy
bodies across the silken cover
of my grandmother's bed,
the quilt stained with brown
shoe polish that I, as a toddler,
found and spilled
on the downy quilt.

My immaculate grandmother kept it,
she said, because when I wasn't there
the comforter reminded her
of me.
It's such a small stain, eh?

I can *feel* yet the severe
girth of her body
entrapped in a bundle of bone,
though love spilled out,
see her as she gardened
so outfitted, burrs
catching on her dark hose
and on the laces of her
no-nonsense shoes.

She needed no corset
to keep her upright.
My grandmother was
as unyielding as the undergarment
she wore, holding firm in her
God, her family and flowers,
her commitment to enfold her grandchild
against her upright bosom.

Though the stays poked
tender skin, I said nothing,
glad to be held by this woman
who corseted me, whose wide arms
ceded just enough to accommodate
one small form.

A Strange Repast

Grandma was a good cook
except
for the molded Jell-O salad she made
every holiday. It was lime green
in color and filled with carrots and celery
and green olives stuffed with pimientos.
(I'm not making this up; check it out online.)

Who would create such a thing?
My cousin, cringing, recalls it as well.
Every Thanksgiving, Jell-O graced
the table, shimmering in the candlelight,
waiting for some brave soul
to dig in.
After my first try, I politely declined,
or worse, took a slice and smashed it
around on my plate
to make it look as though
I had eaten some, fooling no one.
(This was not something you could
feed the dog under the table.)

Why remains the question.
Julia Child must have fainted.
Why didn't someone speak up,
suggest Grandma make a cherry pie
instead of the atrocity
that shook every time
a dish was passed?
Thank God, the tradition
died when she did, though
I will long remember

that molded slop
sitting next to the turkey
and glistening after dinner
on the kitchen counter
while we children silently applauded
its demise, anxious
for the remains to sink
to the depths of the garbage pail,
absent from our lives . . .
until the next year.

Sunday Mornings

Grandma and I would trek
the quarter mile down a country road
to the streetcar,
Grandma dressed for church
in her finest, always wearing
a suit and a hat
even on the hottest summer days.

We'd ride the trolley
to the Erskine Church
where my uncle's photo hung
in the hallway, proof
that Canadians served
proudly in the war.

And the podium
bore a plaque honoring
my grandfather,
dead before I was born.
I'd fidget while the minister
droned on about nothing
of interest to a youngster
eager to be liberated
from the confines
of an hour-long sermon.
Those sermons didn't take.

My favorite part
was the Doxology:
Praise God from whom all blessings flow,
for I knew they'd collect
the money and we'd soon
be released.

Usually some friend
of Grandma's
would drive us home,
where the river
awaited, where the trees
and my pal awaited,
where I was free to enjoy
the true miracles
for yet another week.

A Lesson in Stoicism

The night my grandmother locked
herself in the garage, the back portal
slamming behind her, and she not strong
enough to lift the heavy front door
to freedom, she found a chair,
an old blanket, and settled
in for the evening.

She must have been
in there for hours,
though when we saw the light
and opened the garage, she was
her usual, cheerful self. "I knew
you'd find me eventually," she
said. "The cat kept me company."

When we opened the door,
the cat, who lacked Grandma's
fortitude, bounded out of the garage,
a grumpy look on his face.

Not Grandma.
She smiled at us. "No worries,"
she told us. "I'm fine. And
I learned a thing or two. Always
make sure the door is unlocked."

I learned a thing or two
as well. No one could beat
my grandma as role model.
And when you're locked in
or out, settle down and enjoy
the quiet, the cat on your lap.
Enjoy the music only
you can hear.

Good Neighbors

In the days before *Life Alert,*
the cottage neighbors
placed a buzzer in Grandma's
home, so she could contact
them in an emergency. (As a child
I was warned never to push
That Button. Though tempted, I never did.)

Evenings, we were often invited
over to watch their black-and-white
television, the first in the neighborhood.
Grandma's favorite show
was *Kraft Music Hall.* After
Perry Como enchanted us with his
melodic tunes, we would wander
back to the cottage through the fading light
of Canadian summer evenings, holding hands
so Grandma wouldn't fall on the dirt path,
humming along to the song
still playing in our heads:
"Don't Let the Stars Get in Your Eyes,"
though stars were often in our eyes
those magical years, stars that
shine still, brightening the nights
of my life, brightening the memory
of those summers by the river.

Bringing Her Home

In memory of Susan Rae

The photo says it all.
The young woman carries
her grandmother's
ashes, cradles the urn
in her arms as she walks
past silent neighbors
waving their goodbyes.

Not the ending we wanted,
no memorial
to honor her, though she
remains memorialized
in our hearts: her quick
laugh, her love of children,
her witticisms.

To end like this,
no family or friends
at her side allowed to say
our in-person good-byes,
allowed to kiss the sweet
face that remains now,
in memory, she but one
victim of the mysterious
plague that roams the earth.

She would rail
at the unfairness
of it all, not for
herself, but for the lost,

the poor, the loved ones
denied a hand to hold
at these last moments,
denied one final, poignant
farewell.

The Woodshed

The inside of Grandma's woodshed
smelled of the musty scent of wet wood,
a leaky roof the cause of the fragrance
I loved.

I left the shed door open so the sun
would shine in, so I could read
in the doorway and watch
the black squirrels at their mischief.

The woodshed is long gone, my
dear grandmother the same, yet
the scent comes upon me at times,
in a friend's old storage building,

in our damp woodpile, carrying
me back years to that spot
I shared with Grandma's hoe and rake,
tools to keep the vegetables flourishing,

as I flourished
in that decaying ruin,
loving every minute in my
private playhouse by the river.

Unspoken Love

I wonder
if my grandmother knew
how much she colored
my life,
giving me a childhood
to remember,
giving me ample time
to wander alone
the banks of the Ottawa,
tossing pebbles into the ripples,
tossing questions about the future
into the air.

I never told her
what she meant to me,
children seldom do,
though as an adult
I should have spoken.

But there was one day when
my young son and I visited
with her in the nursing
home, Grandma bed-bound, so I asked,
Do you remember the times we sat
together in the dining room watching
the lightning flash over the water,
listening to the roar
of summer thunder
that shook the cottage?
Do you remember how
we walked each Sunday
past the other cottages
all the way to the streetcar
on the main road
in time to make it to church?

Tears rimmed her eyes
and rolled down her cheeks.
She was beyond speaking, though I know
she heard.

She tried to smile
as we both returned
to an earlier time,
a sacred time
for both.
I held her hand,
comforted her
with memories,
as I comforted myself.

My son, a toddler,
grew restless in the room,
so I kissed that wizened
face, said our good-byes.

How I loved that old woman.

I wonder if she knew.

Geese on a Northern California Pond

For thirty years I heard the cries,
the flap of wings heavier than
air, than the longing of that child
who stood, hand in Grandmother's
hand and watched Canadian skies
dark with your masses, my wonder
carried with you—
to here.

Memory's tint is
silver—
silver wings,
silver waters of the Ottawa,
silver hair, a weave of time
rewoven now in glint of bone,
piece of sky.
Heavy bodied, elegant on pond
or field, this twice-told
gift,
this fine-toothed
love.

Simple Gifts

We wait years
for the pure pleasure
of grandchildren, their first
crooked grins, their eyes
wide with discovery.

Now there's time to listen
to their funny sayings,
write them down, when
we were too busy to do
the same for our own.

"Go potty 'morrow night,"
my two-year-old grandson
tells me. "I don't know
how I fell," my young granddaughter
explains. "Suddenly I just became unstable."

Reminding me of her mother
as a youngster, running into the house
crying: "Mommy, I hurt my knee-bow!"
Reminding me of all the knee-bows
I've bandaged over the years,
all the babes
I've rocked into the future.

Rocked into the now.

Taking Back the Moon

"Grammy," my six-year-old granddaughter asks,
"why do they call it 'the *man* in the moon'?"

Her mother was less than a month old when
we landed on the lunar landscape. I nuzzled soft warm
baby skin and watched as men bounded down a ladder
to the silky surface, left huge footprints in the dust,
stuck a flag in her face.

A woman would have stepped lightly on this ground,
collected moon dust for her child's hair,
swept away her footprints, left nothing.
Not *I came, I saw, I conquered*,
rather, *I visited, I cried, I'll remember*.

In their blood, women remember.

One day this child will learn about the monthly
cycle dependent on the moon
that will tie her for all time to her sisters
and to the sky above.
Time and tide wait for no man, they say,
though the tide waits for women.

Think of the harvest moon.
No *combine* here, but the harvest of old:
putting up preserves, pickles,
jars of jam and jellies canned,
herbs dried for the coming year.

Women did this, gazed at the round
curvy woman-moon and knew
what they saw: not a man
in the heavens but a female face
smiling, transmitting wisdom
through moonbeams to earth,
transmitting forgiveness
for the scars on her surface,
the collection of instruments left
behind that teach us nothing of what
women already know: that mystery
interrupted is still and always mystery
and beyond capture.

Directions to the Good Life

For my grandchildren

Head north to the future, windows
rolled down to collect the breeze.
On your way, feed the hungry.

Gas up on wonder.

Bypass the intersection of bitterness
and anger. Get lost. Find yourself
in kindness and smiles.

Stitching a Life

For a grandchild unborn

The Foundation row: The first
stitch is patience—chain loosely.

Row 2: Slip stitch commitment.
Hook in humor and continue to end.

Next Row: Skip hatred,
and work around bitterness.
Repeat.

Back loop in books,
and dog and cat pals.
Measure in forgiveness,
yarn over prejudice.
Edge with crimson sunrise.

Size with wonder
and dahlias large as dinner plates.
Mark with passion and thunderheads
and music.

Fringe in hopscotch and hikes
in the hills.
Join beach days with friends.

Seam with enthusiasm
and help for the poor.
Repeat.

Gauge with dreams realized,
and tears for tenderness.

Weave in idealism.
Block with laughter
and hammocks and swings.
Hand wash in kindness.

Finish with poetry,
wrapped in a blanket
of your mother's fierce love.

The Quickening

On the eve of the Perseids' rain
of fire
a call arrives:
I felt the baby!
and the excitement
in my daughter's voice
is the same as when she stood
by my bedside at four a.m.
on Christmas morn to squeal,
He's been here!

Thirty years—
as brief as the lives
of the shooting stars
I crane my neck to view
on this night drawing
flame
and the priestly poet
comes to mind—
not kingfishers or dragonflies,
but stars, hallowed light,
and the quickening.

For this I came.

For Aubrey, at One

Fever claims her baby rest
and she lays her small fierce body
against my chest and pats
my back as if to say,
It's okay, Grandma; I know
you had nothing to do
with this.

The wild expanse of years
moves between us—
little miss/crone
bridged by touch
I pat *her* back
to soothe
this child of my child.

As my grandmother
patted me,
her wrinkled hands, so mild,
now mine
breeching time
to bind all three:
Ghost, Grandmother, Child.

T-Rex Rebuke

Hannah, almost two, and I
were enjoying an afternoon reading
on her parents' bed. She snuggled
next to me as we perused one
picture book after another.

Suddenly, my husband, thinking
he was being funny, jumped
into the room and growled his
very best Tyrannosaurus impersonation.

Hannah hurled herself into my lap
while I glared at the offender.
When he made a speedy retreat,
Hannah said to me, "That's a bery bad guy,"
giving me ammunition for the future,
for those occasions when he irritates
me beyond measure.

Now I can look at him when necessary
and announce with conviction
and a certain satisfaction,

"You're a bery bad guy."

From the Mouths of Babes

Hannah was two-and-a-half the Thanksgiving
she gave Morfar (Norwegian for mother's father),
his comeuppance.
They were playing on the living room floor
when the call to dinner came.
"Let's pick up the toys now, Hannah, so we can eat."
Hannah, in typical two-year-old fashion,
said "No." Again, Morfar made his case:
"We need to put the toys away now."
Again, Hannah, still playing, said no.

Morfar, an imposing large man with a booming
voice, bellowed, "Hannah, no one says no to Morfar!"
Hannah stood up, hands on wee hips, looked
at him and responded,
"Grammy does."

More Than His Share

My husband and I
joined my daughter
and her family
for dinner at a restaurant
known for its terrific desserts.

After we finished our meals,
we ordered one large
dish of frozen delicacy,
complete with five spoons.

Back at my daughter's home
I asked my three-year-old
granddaughter how she liked
the ice cream.

She looked at me and shrugged.
"I don't know," she answered.
"Grandpa ate it all."

Saving for College

When my granddaughter
was born,
her parents started
a savings account
for her future schooling.

To aid with that,
a large jar, situated
in a corner of the kitchen,
filled with coins her parents,
friends and relatives
dropped into it.

Periodically,
the family would trek
to the bank to deposit
the offerings.

One day when
I was visiting
I learned
that the container
had shattered.

I asked my granddaughter, then three,
where she thought
we might find a replacement.
She thought a moment, then responded,
"Probably at the college fund store."

In Aubrey's Shadow

It is a warm spring morning, ripe with possibility. I watch as my granddaughter lines up her stuffed animals on the picnic table: Platypus, Chickee, Curious George's child, baby monkey. She adds a doll named J.C. Penney.
"What are you doing, Bug?"
"I'm teaching."
"Oh. Are you teaching algebra?"
"No, I'm teaching *children*. Grammy, pretend I'm pregnant." She hurries to her doll carriage, stuffs a doll under
her shirt, and turns around. "See?"
"I see." She grunts three times, then reaches under
her shirt and delivers her child.
"Wow!" I say. "Easy labor." Aubrey shows me her effort. "That's a beautiful baby," I tell her. "Is it a boy or a girl?"
"It's a girl. Her name is Jennifer."
"I thought you already had a Jennifer."
She thinks about this. "Well, now I have Jennifer One and Jennifer Two."
"Oh," I reply.
"Grammy? Can you spell SPD?" The name of our local market flies out of her mouth.
"I can," I answer.
"Me too. S . . . P . . . D." She laughs and runs off, returning with several small rocks from the garden. "Smell these. Rocks smell good."
I inhale the odor of earth after rain, having forgotten the importance of smelling stones.
"Let's do yoga," she says. On spindly legs Aubrey
assumes the tree pose and almost falls over. "You do it."
I become a tree.
"Now say *Namaste*."
I comply. "No, like this. Say *Namaste* and bow."
She bows.

"Grandma, how old are you?"
"I'm sixty."
There is a pause. "Oh, oh. I'm four."
"I thought you were three."
"Well, I'm not. I'm four. I decided. I'm magic."
With this I agree.
"Grammy, want to see what I have?" She comes
to me and uncups small hands to reveal an imaginary caterpillar.
"Look!" she says. "Let's put it on a tree,
and when we come back, it will turn into a beautiful butterfly." She skips to a Catalpa tree and places her caterpillar on the bark.
She does not know my butterfly is already here, flitting non-stop from one wonder to the next, tap-dancing, hopping,
arms wide to the world, singing "She'll Be Comin 'Round the Mountain," providing me with a second chance to see anew.
"Grammy? Want to jump on the bed?" I consider this. "Okay, but don't tell your mom. Race you to the house," I tell her. Her whole body engages, and she bends for the count. "Okay, Grandma. On your mark, get set . . ."

  Go. Run into the future with this curly-haired child of my child, brown-eyed fairy sprite with wings askew.
Ever so glad.
Grateful.

Why I Am a Vegetarian

The stench
of the feed lot
outside Coalinga
hangs like fog
over Highway 5
and poisons
the air.

What's that smell?
my four-year-old grandson
asks my daughter,
driving the distance
between Nevada City
and LA.
He holds his nose.

Cow poop, she says.
You know, cows?
Hamburgers?

There is silence
from the back seat
while my grandson
stares out the window
at the incarcerated beasts,
and processes this information.
Finally, thoughtfully,
he speaks.
Hamburgers are made
from cow poop?

Family Ties

For years I've moved
banana slugs and salamanders
out of harm's way, placing
them on the sides of trails
to save them from being
stepped on by hikers,
or run over by bike riders,
a small gesture to honor
small creatures.

When I heard the tale
of my four-year-old granddaughter
standing resolute to protect
the yellow mollusk,
I knew family ties
run deep.

One weekend morning
when my granddaughter and her daddy
were walking down their country
lane, they spotted a banana slug.
My son-in-law picked up
the slug, showed his daughter
the creature, had her touch
the damp skin before they
released it to continue its journey.

When they heard a car
approach, my granddaughter
started yelling, gesturing
to the ground. "Don't
run over the banana slug!"
she pleaded. "Don't hit it!"

DNA runs deep.

Almost Here

One Christmas when my daughter's children
were young, she and her family drove north
to spend the holidays with us.

On Christmas Eve, in an attempt to entertain
my five-year-old grandson, I invited him
to watch NORAD tracking Santa's trip
around the globe.

My grandson watched, intrigued, as the internet
revealed Santa's travels through the sky.
When the computer suggested that the reindeer-pulled
sleigh was nearing California, I pointed this out
to Colton. He took a closer look, peering at the screen,
then jumped up, ran to the door, turned around
and said, "I need to go to bed NOW!"

Lies We Tell Children

Hannah Banana, who is five,
traces a line in the sand
with the toe of her Mary Janes—
and, with a look,
dares me to cross over.
I will always be here for you, I tell her.

She has heard this before.

She hasn't read Bettelheim,
can't know the symbolism
of the thin *Beauty and the Beast*
nightgown she wore the morning
she ran barefoot down the street
after my son crying, *Daddy, come back,*
though already she knows I am
frail protection from the real beasts
that devour children.

What fractured beauty, this
child of my child, this
sprite, who hops,
skips a half-skip,
slides her hand
in my hand,
and dares me
to cross over.

The Environmentalist

"What are those men doing?" my five-year-old
granddaughter asks me, watching from the back seat
of the car as a crew from the electric company
sprays paint on trees. "They're marking the trees
to be cut," I respond.

"Those are *horrible* people!" she tells me.
"Birds live in trees. Squirrels live in trees."

"They're not going to cut all of them," I reassure her.
"They'll just cut some branches too close
to the wires so when it's windy the branches don't hit
the wires and start a fire."

She listens, unconvinced. "But," she says,
"We need trees to capture carbon dioxide."

"Is that something you learned in school?" I ask,
fascinated at the information stored in one small brain.

"No, Grandma," she responds. "It's just something I know."

All For One

In third grade my granddaughter
played on two basketball teams,
both coached by her father.

One Saturday as the girls were preparing
for their second game of the day,
my granddaughter announced that she
had forgotten her second-team tee-shirt.
Her father, no doubt attempting
to instill responsibility, told her
that she could not, then, play.
Grandma at the ready, I offered
to retrieve the shirt for her.
He shook his head.

A half-dozen eight-year-olds
listened to this conversation.
After a moment, one stood up
and announced: "Coach, if Aubrey's
not playing, I'm not either."
Then another one stood. "Me neither."
To a girl they stood together.
Realizing he would have to forfeit
the game, Coach relented and
a proper tee-shirt was found.

"In time responsibility will come,"
I told him. "The good news
is you have proof that you have
created a unified team."

They won the game.

Dentist Appointment

My granddaughter fears the bright lights,
the masks,
the metal tools that
scrape against her tiny teeth.

Poked by too many
white-coated strangers,
this child fears
being touched
by more

and so stiffens,
makes a plank
of her body,
becomes an impenetrable
frozen form.

A bribe, the promise
of a gift long awaited,
thaws her
enough that
she accommodates
the chair, though
she does not
relinquish her ironing-board
pose.

The dentist, honoring
this one small person,
is patient,
speaks softly to her,
shows her the mirror.
Her terror recedes
by inches.

Tears roll down
her reddened cheeks,
though she makes no sound.
Instead, she grips the armrests,
understanding the nature of objects
that do not give.

Equine Love

Chloe on horseback
transforms from a gangly teenager
to a vision of perfection,
at one with her mount.

Together they brave the jump,
the girl, centered, focused,
the horse, measuring
the distance.

They glide—for an instant airborne—
then return to earth
together, beast not missing stride
and girl, aglow.

It is here
where she achieves,
here, where she forgets
for a time her adolescent angst.

If only she could stay atop
her horse love, cantering
her way onward, loping
through life with her four-legged friend.

Walkaway

The eleven-year-old daughter
who walked ahead of me,
pretended she didn't know
me, is here
again.

Many years later, another
eleven-year-old, her mother's form
revisited,
pretends we're not related,
shoulders her backpack,
answers my
queries with one-word
responses, bored
beyond words
by my attempts
to connect.

Twice in one lifetime
I witness the separation,
the bid for independence
and recall my own
parent I pretended
at the same age not to know.

How cruel we are at eleven,
breaking hearts,
not knowing that
the heart we break
will one day be
our own.

The Test of Time

My eighteen-year-old granddaughter
proudly lifts her shirt
to reveal a tattoo
that travels from her stomach
around her side
and up her back to her shoulder blades.

Despite my understanding of scarification
rituals, of rites of passage,
I am struck numb at the sight.

Age gives us some things,
so what I say—when I finally
catch my breath—is,
Wow! That must have really hurt!

But what I want to say is,
When you're sixty . . .

*When you're sixty,
that flower-arrangement thing
around your navel is going to look like
Morning Glories after a hard frost.*

*And those fairies with wings akimbo
alighting so airily
on a tendril or two?
Their wings are going to droop.*

*You think Tinker Bell
is ageless, don't you, kid?
Don't fool yourself. She's
really, really old,
probably even has age spots.*

Am I missing something here,
a new archetype
known only to the young?
A symbol, perhaps,
I'm just not getting?
Vines. Okay, youth, new beginnings.
Pain as transformative experience?
But isn't there enough pain in life
already?

Is it the art itself?
Some guy with needles and colored ink
transforming your body
into his masterpiece
only a very few—I hope—
will see?

What will you tell
your children?
How will they
up the ante—and they will—
on this?

I'm too old.
Bring back the days
of innocence: of rock 'n' roll
and poodle skirts,
a time when tattoos
were seen only on sailors
or ex-cons.

A time when young women
necked a bit, partook
in serious groping in the back
seat of a '59 Ford, promised
love everlasting to the boy
who copped a feel.
But love and only love
was the excuse for presenting,
for revealing, tender young skin
so fresh in its beauty
to another.

A time when grandmas' lips
pinched at the sight
of a too-tight blouse on their granddaughters'
chests and didn't hesitate
to speak their piece,
to chastise a child
who violated unwritten codes
of womanhood.

It was all so clear then—
lines of demarcation
one dared not trespass.

Art had its place in museums,
in nature,
not on the backs of children.

Climbing Mount Hope

For Hannah

It's a trek, isn't it, this journey into territory found on no map.
Uncharted land, often barren. Boulders everywhere.
Altitude sickness? Nothing to what you've faced.
The threat of avalanche. Imagine that ride, the whoosh of wind,
the call of birds amazed to see you fly, the white snow
perfect on a far-off hill.

You press on, latitude unknown. At this height,
weak sun bathes the landscape.

At the crest, clouds mask the horizon.
In the fading light, you come upon a flag
of many colors, a note attached. It reads:
Advice from a Fellow Traveler, One Who Loves You.
Dress warmly.
Take your meds.
Yell at the indifferent moon.
Enjoy the view, however fleeting.
Keep climbing.
Call home.

The Grandmother I Never Knew

In the one photo
I have of my mother's mother,
she is holding me, an infant
of three or four months,
while my three-year-old brother
stands beside us.

We are outdoors at her home
on Bear Lake, in the bush country
of central Ontario.

Years later I learned
that my grandmother cared
for me until she became ill,
at which point my mother's
best friend, also living in a small
Ontario town, took me in,
while my mother returned
to Toronto, to the husband
who was not my father.

How often I've wondered
about that grandmother—
what she thought of her daughter,
one of five children—what
she thought when she learned
I had been adopted.

My cousin, found a few years ago,
told me that our grandmother
loved gardening and playing
board games with her.

But was there an ache,
a feeling of loss,
for that infant she once held?

When I learned she was the first
in their small village to sow
California poppies, I smiled,
for I like to think she planted
them in remembrance of the child
who disappeared so many years before
to California.

Every year,
I scatter poppy seeds
to grace the flower beds,
the hillsides, to honor
the grandmother I never knew.

A Grace Note

In memory of my children's grandmother, Damaris Rae

She was competent
and committed,
compassionate
and caring,

easing
a squalling babe
from crib
to rock away the tears.
So many babes.

She was compassionate,
gathering goods
for her church's
food cupboard,
sharing, always
thinking of others.

She was committed,
bringing her faith
to a Lenten desert
protest at a Nevada
nuclear test site,
where she was arrested,
this gentle supporter
of environmental causes.

She was competent,
raising five children
on little money,
though much love, sewing
their clothes, her
homespun ways
a gift.

She knew the birthdays
of her sixteen grandchildren,
gifted them all
with home-made doll clothes,
perhaps a baseball glove
for a young Little Leaguer.

She was taken
too soon, an unassuming
woman who touched
so many.

In honor, her church choir
sang the "Hallelujah Chorus"
at her memorial, her favorite music,
even though she passed
in October.

Damaris, like the music
she so loved,
was a grace note
in our lives.

Sweeping Up a Life

I make piles: *the mistakes,*
like dust motes under the couch,
escape in a breeze
of delusion, then settle
on a floor of truth.

Pile two: *regrets,*
large, but workable
and beyond excuse.

Pile three: *proud moments,*
a few, my children and their
children, the call of "Grandma"
echoing down the hall.

Pile four: *love,*
that shimmers off my life
like sunlight on the pines:
My man, friends,
a cat asleep in a shaft
of sunlight, the dog
on the porch.
Birds, always birds,
a garden of surprises,
and the sweet vibrant
hum of insects
applauding the dawn.

What We Have Wrought

For all the grandchildren

Forgive us, sweet persons,
for what we have wrought.
It was not our intent,
in fact, we sought
a better world for you.

But in our ignorance,
and in our greed,
we hurt the earth
and sowed the weeds
of destruction.
Hurricanes, tornadoes,
drought and flame,
dead coral reefs,
we take the blame
for what

we have sown:
lead in the water,
plastic in the seas.
If only we had known
the destruction ahead.

Can you forgive us?
We'll work to repair,
to restore, to renew.
We'll do it for Earth,
we'll do it for you.

Forgive us our ignorance,
forgive us our greed.
We did not listen,
we did not heed
the signs.

We leave you hope,
we leave you love.
We leave you faith
that the stars above
will guide you

to create a better world
than the one we left
you, the one we maimed.

Forever saddened.
Forever shamed.

Two Gardeners

An old woman,
a child,
garden together in silence,
tend the earth, pulling
weeds, watering
the cabbage,
(though the child
does not like cabbage).

Instead she gathers
raspberries, putting
as many in her mouth
as in the bowl.

Her grandmother nods,
smiles, and continues
the tasks at hand, giving
back to the soil that feeds them.

Years later, the girl,
a grandmother now herself,
will recall that sacred land
at the cottage,
will think of the woman
who taught her to love
gardens, merely by nodding,
by smiling, by saying
little.

Turn of Hand

The perfume of Carolina Jessamine
wafting through drawn shades on a still summer
afternoon
is the same scent
my grandmother admired,
worked her hands in earth
as I do.
The light, the feel
of moist black dirt
moves behind drawn years
and the sorrow is
a fragile bond so fine
I can reach out and touch my grandmother's hands—
lined, caked with mud thick beneath torn nails
yellowed as her braids,
can hear still
the crack of hard-shelled cucumber beetles
she crushed between thumb and index finger.

My grandmother is
hot earth,
the blood of offending beetles
and Carolina Jessamine so abundant
it lingers on air so thick
I wear it,
become my
grandmother working soil,
tugging at roots
so embedded
they stretch beyond
California clay
all the way to my grandmother's home
three thousand miles, three thousand sorrows
and a childhood away.

About the Author

Judie Rae is the author of the novel *The Haunting of Walter Rabinowitz*. Her poems have appeared in many literary journals and anthologies, among them *Nimrod, Wisconsin Review,* and *Mudfish*. She is the author of two chapbooks, *The Weight of Roses* and *Howling Down the Moon*. She is the co-editor of *Old Age & Young Hearts,* a chapbook written by women over sixty. Her essays have appeared in "Tahoe Quarterly," "The Sacramento Bee," as well as online at San Francisco's NPR station, KQED. Judie taught college English classes for twenty-seven years at various colleges throughout California. A Canadian, she now lives in Nevada City, Ca., a landscape reminiscent of her grandmother's home on the Ottawa River, where Judie spent her childhood summers.

www.ingramcontent.com/pod-product-compliance
Lightning Source LLC
Chambersburg PA
CBHW071332190426
43193CB00041B/1756